W9-DGJ-986

When Dragons' Hearts were Good

Master Books

When Dragons' Hearts were Good

by Buddy Davis

illustrated by Dan Lietha

Master
Books

A Division of New Leaf Press

First printing: June 1999

ISBN: 0-89051-259-0
Library of Congress Number: 99-64018

Cover by Janell Robertson
Illustrations by Dan Lietha

Printed in the United States of America

Introduction

Dragons are often used as symbols of evil. In our book you'll experience these created animals differently. With Bible teaching applied from the Book of Genesis, the first book of the Bible, we hope this story will minister to you and entertain you and your children.

The story is obviously a fictional account of what life may have been like in the Garden of Eden, before Adam sinned. It is based on the facts about the history of creation found in Genesis.

This special book comes with a CD which includes the original song "When Dragons' Hearts Were Good," which inspired the story. Buddy Davis, the author and musician, reads the story, complete with sound effects, for your enjoyment. If you would like a copy of the sheet music for the song, arranged for both piano and guitar, please visit either of our websites at: www.masterbooks.net or www.answersingenesis.org.

We trust you'll treasure this story as you experience first hand When Dragons' Hearts Were Good.

G LORIOUS! WONDERFUL! MAGNIFICENT! SPECTACULAR! Adam and Eve were excited as they explored God's creation, the perfect Garden of Eden. It was a beautiful garden that God himself had planted. They enjoyed eating the ripe, delicious fruits and vegetables that God had growing all around them. This very special garden was also full of friendly animals, birds, insects, and reptiles — even dragons!

Adam and Eve spent the day walking and running through the garden. There were new adventures at every turn. While they took care of this special garden they often stopped to admire a fragrant flower swaying gently in the breeze or to listen as a colorful bird chirped a song of praise to its Creator. Vines hanging from the limbs of the trees made swings on which monkeys and parrots played. The dragons loved their animal neighbors, and the other animals loved the dragons, too.

God gave Adam and Eve some important rules to obey in the Garden. They obeyed God, and every creature on earth was happy and everything was very good. The garden of Eden was perfect!

A dam and Eve loved to hold hands as they walked through the garden in the cool of the evening. The dragons liked to follow Adam and Eve and breathe fire into the night air.* The fire would light the path for them as they walked and talked to their Creator for hours into the night.

*Note for parents: The many dragon stories (often in remarkable detail) around the world clearly speak of a time when people saw live dinosaurs. These often have the dragon emitting "fire and smoke." See also Job chapter 41, the description of the fierce leviathan. Biologically, there is no reason why some (now extinct) creatures may not have had this feature. The living bombardier beetle, for example, "blasts" its enemies with a jet of heat from a chemical reaction akin to an explosion.

Awakened by the songbirds at daybreak, the two dragons wasted no time as they leaped from the nest inside their cozy den. Instantly, they pounced on each other, and the game was on. They playfully wrestled and chased each other in circles through the morning mist that rose from the ground. The sounds of the dragons as they frolicked carried through the garden and woke Adam and Eve.

Adam and Eve peered through the wildflowers looking for the noisemakers. Eve started to giggle as she spied the dragons playing tag. "That looks like fun," Adam shouted as he ran to join them. What a way to start the day!

That was before Adam sinned.
The earth was perfect way back then.

I'd restore the garden if I could,
When even dragons' hearts were good.

There were many different kinds of dragons in God's newly created paradise. Some were giants like the long-necked behemoths. The triceratops had three horns and a shield on their heads. They used their heads to butt fruit trees and shake down the tasty treats.

One of the strangest-looking pair of dragons, the stegosaurs, had triangular-shaped plates which grew out from their back along the spine. When they wanted to be warm, they would stand in the rays of the greater light and let the sunbeams shine on their plates to warm their huge bodies. When they wanted to be cool, the dragons would stand in the shade of the trees and moved their plates like huge fans. Adam and Eve were amazed at the detail God put into the design of each dragon.

Sharp teeth and claws were not feared in those days. They were only used to slice and chew the bountiful fruits and vegetables that the animals ate. Dragons, bears, big cats like lions, eagles, and animals like cattle and sheep all ate plants and lived in harmony with one another. Even the mighty dragon T-Rex was as gentle as a lamb. Cockatoos would perch on the back of the gentle T-Rex and enjoy the rocking, swaying ride.

The Garden of Eden was alive with the delightful sounds of many different animals. As Adam was feeding one of the dragons, he heard a noise overhead. He looked up and saw another kind of dragon gliding effortlessly through the sky. It was a flying dragon named Pteranodon. Perhaps Adam and Eve even dreamed of riding on these huge, flying dragons, clinging tightly to their backs and listening to the sound of their large wings whistling through the air!

That was before Adam sinned.

The earth was perfect way back then.

I'd restore the garden if I could.

When even dragons' hearts were good.

I am sorry to have to tell you, but sin would soon change everything in God's creation. We sin when we disobey God's rules. It wouldn't be long before Adam and Eve would disobey God by breaking His rules.

Their sin would cause all God's perfect creation to become corrupt. It wouldn't be perfect anymore. God would have to punish them and would make them leave His beautiful garden forever.

Long shadows began to creep into the garden as they neared the end of another day. Fireflies gave off a soft yellow glow.

It was during the evening that God, the Creator of heaven and earth, talked with His two special friends in the garden. As the three walked together, God explained to Adam and Eve that they were created differently than the animals. They weren't animals, they were made in God's own image!

Adam and Eve were the two most beautiful and intelligent people the world has ever known. Out of all God's creation, they were His favorites. In fact, He loved them so much that in the future, to pay for their sin (and yours and mine) He would give His Son, Jesus, to die for them (and you and me)!

Adam and Eve must have asked God dozens of questions as they walked. God taught them things that they would pass on to their sons and daughters. As they listened to the voice of their Almighty Creator God, they humbly worshiped Him. The world has never known such joy, happiness, love, or such peace since then.

Soon it was time for God to bid Adam and Eve goodbye for the evening. As they waved goodnight they thought about all that He had taught them. After all, they were learning from the Creator of the universe.

The next day, Adam was watching a small spider weave a silky web among the stems of some plants. He marveled as the small gopher tree seeds fell into the sticky web and provided a good meal for the fuzzy spider that nibbled at them.

"Company's coming," said Eve, smiling. She pointed toward the two dragons that were approaching. They greeted Adam and Eve with a friendly lick. The dragons then laid their heads on Adam's lap and purred in contentment as Eve gently stroked their backs.

As Adam and Eve relaxed in God's paradise, they looked up at a clear blue sky. Everything worked together in perfect harmony. God created the world and it was very good. Adam and Eve hadn't disobeyed God's rules by eating the forbidden fruit from the tree of the knowledge of good and evil yet. It was a land before the rainbow; a land before tears were true.

That was before Adam sinned.
The earth was perfect way back then.

36

God will restore the earth someday.
Children will laugh with dragons as they play.

God will restore the heavens and the earth one day! Then it will be as it was in the Garden of Eden. The wolf will live with the lamb, and the calf and the young lion will live together in peace. The beast of the wild will be led by a child. What a day that will be! There will be no more disease or death, sorrow or pain. If we receive Jesus as our Savior, He will wipe the tears from our eyes and we will be forever with Him. Perhaps we will be able to play with the dragons, just as Adam and Eve did, because in heaven, even dragons' hearts will be good.

THE END

When Adam and Eve disobeyed God by eating the forbidden fruit, sin entered the world. God is Holy and can have no part of sin. It must have made Him very sad to expel His two friends from the garden. Because of sin, death, disease, and suffering entered our world. Sin not only affects our world but the Bible tells us that the whole creation groans because of sin. Since we are all related to Adam and Eve, we inherit their sin nature (1 Cor. 15:20–22). God's Word tells us that all have sinned and fallen short of the glory of God. That includes you and me.

God loves people so much that He provided a plan of salvation to Adam and Eve before He made them leave the Garden of Eden. That plan was carried out when Jesus Christ, the Creator and Son of God, gave His life for us. He died on a cross, but He arose from the dead. "For God so loved the world, that He gave His only begotten Son, that whosoever believeth in Him should not perish, but have everlasting life" (John 3:16). This means that anyone who believes on Him and receives Him into their lives, becomes a child of God and will live for eternity with the Creator in heaven. "If we confess our sins, He is faithful and just to forgive us our sins, and to cleanse us from all unrighteousness" (1 John 1:9).